MW01234228

THIS NOTEBOOK BELONGS TO:

Made in the USA
Coppell, TX
09 December 2023

25712076R00066